good answers
to tough questions

About Weight Problems
and Eating Disorders

Written by Joy Berry

 CHILDRENS PRESS ®

CHICAGO

Managing Editor: Cathy Vertuca
Copy Editors: Annette Gooch, Cheri Lieurance
Contributing Editors: Joan Price, Melanie Williams,
Jeannine Garczynski, James Gough, M.D.

Art Direction: Communication Graphics
Designer: Jennifer Wiezel
Illustration Designer: Bartholomew
Inking Artist: Alyson Butler
Lettering Artist: Linda Hanney
Coloring Artist: Alyson Butler
Typography and Production: Communication Graphics

Published by Childrens Press
in cooperation with Living Skills Press

This book can answer questions about:
- Wrong Approaches to Creating a Perfect Body
- Creating a Perfect Body
    - Food
    - Proper Eating Habits
    - Water
    - Air and Sunshine
    - Aerobic Exercise
    - Rest and Sleep
- Weight Problems and Eating Disorders
    - Nervous Eating
    - Compulsive Eating
    - Overeating
    - Bingeing
    - Excessive Dieting
    - Bulimia
    - Anorexia nervosa

Many people would like to have a perfect body.

Some people try to make their bodies perfect by deciding exactly how much they should weigh. Then they try to make themselves weigh that amount by losing or gaining weight.

Trying to make yourself weigh what you or someone else thinks you should weigh will not give you a perfect body. Any guess about what you should weigh will most likely be incorrect because no one has found a way to decide precisely how much a person should weigh.

Some people try to decide what the perfect body for them is by comparing themselves with someone whose body they admire. Then they try to make themselves look like the other person.

Trying to make yourself look like someone else will not give you a perfect body.

The body that is perfect for you does not look like any other person's body. You have a one-of-a-kind body that only you were born to have.

Two factors help determine what your one-of-a kind body should look like.

Your **genetic makeup** is the kind of genes you have in your body. A gene is the part of each cell that determines what characteristics a person inherits from his or her parents. Your genetic makeup helps determine your physical size, shape, and appearance.

Your **metabolic rate** is the rate at which your body burns fat. If you have a high metabolic rate, you will tend to burn fat instead of storing it in your body. If you have a low metabolic rate, you will tend to store fat instead of burning it.

You were born with your own genetic makeup and your own metabolic rate.

Your genetic makeup and metabolic rate are not like any other person's. This is why you have a body that is not like any other person's body.

So, the body that is perfect for you will naturally be different in size and shape from the bodies of other people, even if they are your same age.

Creating a perfect body is like raising a perfect plant. To grow a perfect plant, you need to give it the right amount of everything it needs to grow and survive.

If you do this, you will have a plant that is not exactly like any other plant in the world. However, it will be healthy and beautiful in its own way. It will be **perfect**.

To create a body that is perfect for you, you need to give it the right amount of everything it needs to grow and survive.

If you do this, you will have a body that is not like any other body in the world. However, it will be healthy and beautiful in its own way. It will be perfect for you.

Eating good food can help you have a perfect body.

Your body needs the right amount of **carbohydrates**. Carbohydrates give your body energy.

Here are some foods that provide carbohydrates: whole-grain foods, fruit, and vegetables.

Your body needs the right amount of **protein**. Protein helps your body grow and become strong. Protein also helps your body stay well.

Here are some foods that provide protein: fish, poultry, lean meat, milk, cheese, eggs, and certain grains, beans, and peas.

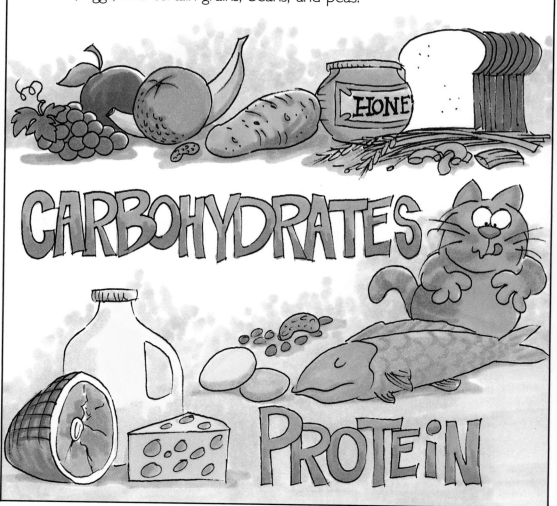

Your body needs the right amount of **unsaturated fats**. These fats are a source of energy for your body and are important in making your body's hormones. Fats also keep your skin smooth and healthy.

Here are some foods that provide unsaturated fats: fish, beans, corn, nuts, and olive oil.

Your body needs the right amount of **fiber**. Fiber helps your body digest (break down) its food and work properly. Fiber also helps keep your teeth clean and your gums healthy.

Here are some foods that provide fiber: raw fruits, vegetables, and whole grain cereals.

FATS

OIL

MAYONNA

ICE

BUTTER

NOTHING ON THIS PAGE LOOKS GOOD TO ME!

OAT BRAN

FiBER

Your body needs the right amount of **vitamins**. Vitamins help your body grow and work properly. They also help your body resist certain diseases and heal quickly.

Here are some foods that are rich in vitamins: milk, eggs, whole-grain foods, yeast, fruits, vegetables, lean meat, fish, and nuts.

Your body needs the right amount of **minerals**. Minerals help your body form strong teeth and bones. They also help your body work properly.

Here are some foods that provide minerals: milk, cheese, eggs, lean meat, fish, dried fruits, and vegetables (especially the green leafy ones).

Too much of some foods, such as sugar, salt, and fat, can hurt your body rather than help it.

"Junk food," such as soda, candy, pastries, cookies, cake, and sugary cereals, have a lot of sugar, salt, or fat in them. Avoid eating these foods.

If you have a difficult time avoiding sweet foods, your body might lack zinc, an important mineral. A zinc deficiency causes a craving for sweets. You can overcome a zinc deficiency by taking a zinc food supplement or by eating foods that contain zinc, such as poultry, tuna, cheese, lentils, nuts, or oats.

Artificial sweeteners can also cause a craving for sweets, so you should avoid using them or eating foods that contain them.

To make sure your body is getting the right amount of good foods, you need to eat the following every day:
- 2 fruits (one should be a citrus fruit, such as an orange)
- 2 vegetables (one should be a dark green or deep yellow)
- 3 or more cups of skim milk (or servings of other foods high in calcium, such as green vegetables)
- 2 or more servings of cheese, eggs, lean meat, fish, poultry, beans, or peas
- 4 or more servings of whole-grain foods

Eating properly can help you have a perfect body. To eat properly, you need to do the following:

- Sit down whenever you eat. Avoid "eating on the run."
- Eat to nourish your body, not to reward yourself or to make yourself feel better.
- Have your breakfast, lunch, dinner, and snack at approximately the same time every day.
- Eat only when you are hungry.
- Eat slowly.
- Chew your food thoroughly before you swallow it.
- Stop eating when you feel full, even if some food remains on your plate.

Drinking enough water can help you have a perfect body.

Water helps keep your body's temperature even so your body does not get too hot or too cold.

Your body consists mostly of water. Every day your body loses water when you urinate and sweat. You need to replace the water so your body can live and stay healthy.

To make sure your body is getting enough water, drink several glassfuls every day. Drink more water on warm days and when you are especially active.

Getting the right amount of fresh air and sunshine can help you have a perfect body.

Air provides the oxygen your body needs to change food into energy.

Sunshine provides the vitamin D your body needs to make strong teeth and bones and to stay healthy. Sunshine also helps you feel better emotionally.

To make sure your body is getting enough fresh air and sunshine, work and play outside as often as possible. Remember to wear a sunscreen, a protective cream that helps prevent sunburn. Too much exposure to the sun can cause you to develop skin cancer when you are older.

Exercising can help you have a perfect body.

Exercise keeps your muscles in good condition so your body can move and function properly. It also helps strengthen your body and keep it flexible.

Exercise helps your blood and other body fluids carry food and oxygen to every part of your body.

Aerobic exercise (exercise that increases your heart rate and oxygen intake) helps burn unwanted fat. It makes you feel energetic and less tired. It also helps you rest and sleep soundly.

To be effective, aerobic exercise should
- increase your breathing and heart rate,
- continue for at least 20 to 30 minutes,
- include both "warm-up" (stretching) and "cool-down" (relaxing) exercises, and
- be done at least three or four times a week.

Here are some activities that provide aerobic exercise: aerobic dancing, running, jogging, fast walking, uphill hiking, jumping rope, bicycling (at least 12 miles per hour), full-court basketball, rowing, swimming, and cross-country skiing.

"Stop and go" activities, such as tennis, handball, racquetball, football, baseball, downhill skiing, and weight lifting, might not provide aerobic exercise.

Getting enough rest and sleep can help you have a perfect body.

Rest and sleep give your body time to repair itself and grow.

Rest and sleep allow your body to build up energy. Without enough rest and sleep, you are more likely to become sick or to injure yourself.

To make sure your body is getting enough rest and sleep,
- take time during the day to rest your body whenever it feels tired, and
- sleep at least nine or ten hours every night.

Perfect bodies are neither **overweight** nor **underweight**.

An overweight body has too much fat on it.

Being extremely overweight can cause the following problems:
- low self-esteem (bad feelings about yourself)
- feelings of shame and guilt about eating
- depression (feelings of sadness or helplessness)
- difficulty in breathing
- difficulty in exercising
- difficulty in moving
- heart problems
- high blood pressure
- diabetes (a disease that affects the body's ability to properly break down and use carbohydrates)

Some people develop eating disorders that cause their bodies to become overweight.

Eating disorders that cause a person to become overweight are
* nervous eating,
* compulsive eating,
* overeating, and
* bingeing.

Nervous eating can cause a person to become overweight. Nervous eating is eating to calm down or feel better.

People who eat nervously often
- eat without being hungry,
- eat when anxious or upset, and
- eat when unhappy.

Nervous eaters often need help from a professional counselor to solve their problems so they can stop eating nervously.

Compulsive eating can cause a person to become overweight. Compulsive eating is eating because of an irresistible urge to do so, not because of hunger.

People who eat compulsively often
- feel out of control,
- eat without being hungry,
- eat without realizing what they are doing, and
- eat continually throughout the day.

Compulsive eaters often need help from a professional counselor to stop eating compulsively.

Overeating can cause a person to become overweight. Overeating is eating more food than is necessary to nourish the body.

People who overeat often
- eat quickly,
- eat large bites,
- eat larger than normal portions of food, and
- eat after feeling full or satisfied.

Overeaters often need help from a professional counselor to stop overeating.

Bingeing can cause a person to become overweight. Bingeing is out-of-control eating of a lot of food at one time.

People who binge often
- eat quickly,
- eat without enjoying it,
- eat until all the food is gone, and
- are secretive about their bingeing.

People who binge often need help from a professional counselor to stop bingeing.

An underweight body does not have enough fat on it.

Being extremely underweight can cause the following problems:

- low self-esteem
- depression
- tiredness
- weakness
- feeling cold, no matter what the temperature
- inability to resist illnesses and infections

Some people develop eating disorders that cause their bodies to become underweight.

Eating disorders that cause a person to become underweight are
- excessive dieting,
- bulimia, and
- anorexia nervosa.

Excessive *dieting* can cause a person to become underweight. Dieting is depriving oneself of foods that can create fat and/or taking in less food than normal.

People who diet excessively often
- think and talk constantly about losing weight,
- follow overly strict eating rules,
- make food the focus of their lives, and
- feel deprived and less fortunate than people who are not dieting.

Dieting is excessive if it keeps the body from getting the food it needs to work properly.

Excessive dieting can eventually cause people to *gain* unwanted weight.

When someone tries to lose unwanted weight by dieting, the body reacts as if it were being starved. When the person stops dieting and starts eating normally, his or her body turns the food into fat and stores it. The body does this to make sure it will not starve if the person starts dieting again.

Bulimia can cause a person to become underweight. Bulimia is bingeing followed by purging (forcing the body to get rid of food it has eaten).

People who are bulimic often
- become extremely fearful of gaining weight,
- follow very strict eating rules that often result in an unbalanced diet,
- force themselves to vomit after eating, and
- take medication (like diuretics and laxatives) to cause themselves to urinate or have bowel movements.

Bulimia can cause the following problems:
- moodiness,
- depression,
- tiredness, or
- dependence upon laxatives.

Continued, forced vomiting due to bulimia can cause the following problems:
- tooth decay,
- throat damage,
- swollen glands,
- damage to the stomach.

Bulimic people often need medical help to overcome bulimia.

Anorexia nervosa can cause a person to become underweight. Anorexia nervosa is eating such small amounts of food that the body cannot work properly.

People who are anorexic often
- think their bodies are fat when they are actually dangerously thin,
- fear gaining even a few pounds,
- eat only very small portions of low-calorie food, and
- exercise too often and too hard.

Anorexia nervosa can cause the following problems:
- moodiness,
- depression,
- excessive worry,
- hyperactivity (excessive activity), and
- insomnia (inability to sleep).

Anorexia nervosa can also cause these problems:
- dry, cold skin,
- bloating,
- stomach cramps,
- digestive problems, and
- slow or irregular heartbeat.

Extreme anorexia nervosa can even lead to death because some parts of the body, such as the heart and kidneys, are so damaged by the lack of food.

Anorexic people often need medical help to overcome anorexia nervosa.

You can avoid weight problems and eating disorders if you
- eat good food,
- eat properly,
- drink enough water,
- get plenty of fresh air and sunshine,
- do aerobic exercise, and
- get enough rest and sleep.

By doing these things, you can have a body that is perfect for you, one that is healthy and beautiful in its own special way.